THE KIRK BY THE TYNE

By

GERALD URWIN

ACKNOWLEDGEMENTS

The author owes a substantial debt to those who assisted in the preparation of this book, including-

The library staff at the John Gray Centre, Haddington,

Ruth Fyfe, archivist,

David Elder who took the photographs in St Mary's,

the staff at East Register House, Edinburgh, and

Martin Ritchie, assistant minister at St Mary's.

GLOSSARY

Merk – two thirds of a Scots pound

Sasine- the act or procedure of giving of feudal property

Beltane – an old Scottish quarter day (1st or 3rd May).

CONTENTS

Part One – Page 10

Part Two – Page 33

Part Three – Page 66

Conclusion – Page 81

PICTURES

Page 5 – Mediaeval interior of St Mary's

Page 27 – Sir James Wilsford

Page 35 – John Knox

Page 58 – The Church interior restored

Page 60 – St Mary's in its ruined state

Page 74 – St Mary's today

AUTHOR'S NOTE.

In 1139 Ada de Warrenne was granted the Burgh Charter of Haddington by her husband. She went further by establishing a Cistercian Abbey on the banks of the Tyne.

St Martin's was also built about this time. On or about 1375 the building of another church was begun, also on the banks of the Tyne. This was St. Mary's as we know it today.

"Where are the words to express

Such a reckless bestowing?

The voices of birds utter less

Than the thanks we are owing.

Bell notes alone

Ring praise of their own

As clear as the weed-weaving brook

And as evenly flowing."

John Betjeman

The early years of St Mary's, Haddington

PART ONE

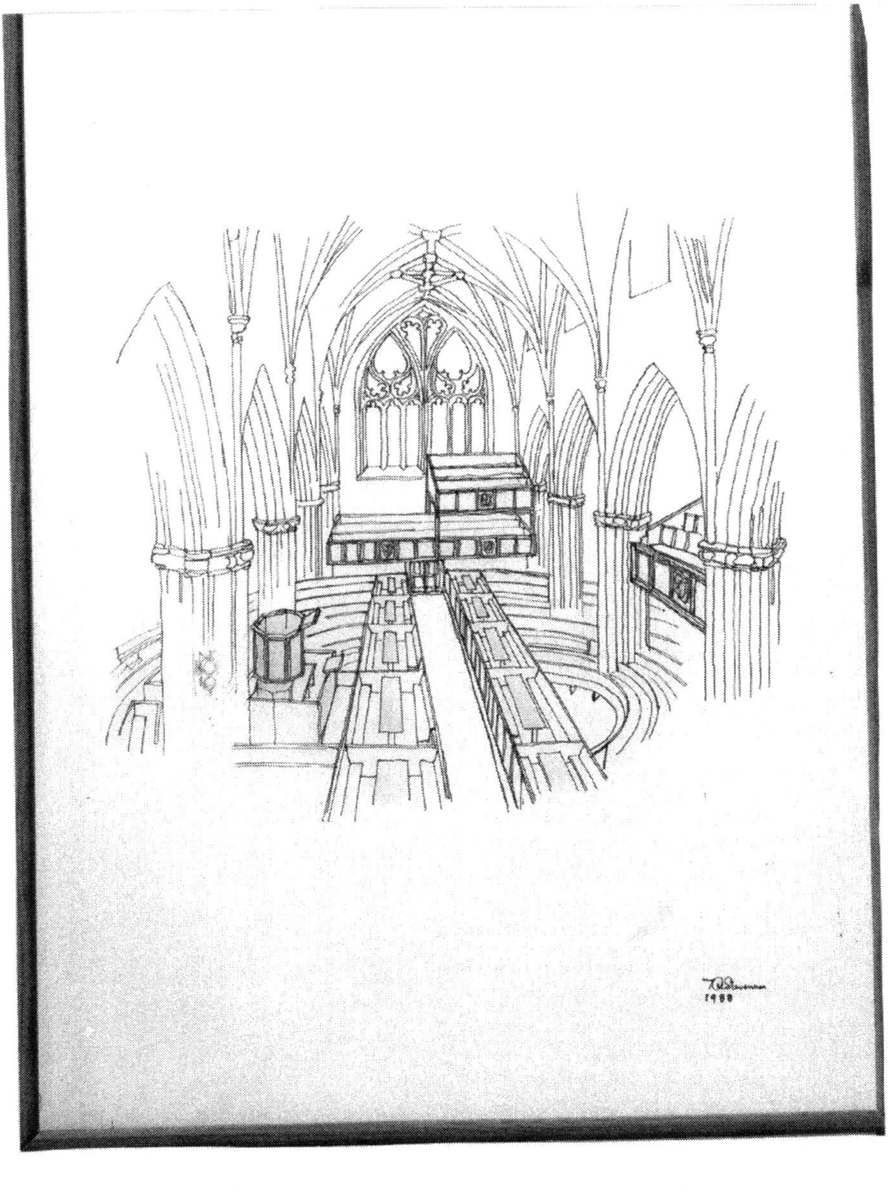

PART ONE – 1420-1549

A visitor to St Mary's Collegiate Church in Haddington, at any time other than a Sunday morning when it is full of worshippers, cannot fail to be impressed with the soaring grandeur of its interior. Some unknown architect has offered a sublime creation in homage to the Lord Divine. It is by far the largest building in the whole of East Lothian, reflecting its importance to the local populace of the time, to whom religion was a constant companion and the true backbone of their very existence.

Their lives were devoted to the upkeep of their precious church. Down the centuries the words of successive Clerks to the Council come to us with reports and instructions concerning St. Mary's. Their names are William Harpar (1423-1450), Alexander Clark (1450-1463), Alexander Simpson (Elder)- (?-1529), Lowrie Flemyng (1533-1539) and Alexander Simpson (Younger) –(1539-1544). Each of them expressed the wishes of the Council of the day in seeing that altars were maintained in good order, that ministers were appointed and that miscreants were punished.

All was to change following the Siege of Haddington 1548-9.

There was a startling contrast between attitudes towards religious participation in church practice in the fifteenth, sixteenth and seventeenth centuries. St Mary's stood, more or less, aloof from the tumult outside while continuing to welcome worshippers.

The early years were dominated by Roman Catholicism. They featured a population totally in awe of the ministry within the Church. Everyone professed belief in the Christian vision on offer, the vision which Roman Catholicism portrayed. Anyone who dared to express any doubts was in danger of being classed as a heretic. If they persisted in their disbelief they risked suffering the same fate as George Wishart, a preacher and proponent of Protestantism who was burnt at the stake.

People attended church service to seek reassurance. In a world where political upheaval was waiting just around the corner to wreak physical devastation and disaster, the church alone could calm those frantic with worry while enjoying mass. Preachers assured them of benefits to be granted. Food would be ever present on the table. Eyesight would never fade. Angels would protect them wherever they were. A total belief in the Word was all important therefore.

Towards the middle of the sixteenth century attitudes began change. Questions were raised and fingers pointed at those officers of a Church who placed themselves at the top of the social ladder. Accusations of overblown pomp and unseemly arrogance were lodged against bishops in particular. In addition, word was coming from Europe of a new belief where "protesters" against the current practice of Roman Catholicism, as witnessed in St Mary's and all other churches throughout the land, offered a different, more acceptable approach. Foremost among these "protestors" was a local man, John Knox, who was born in Giffordgate, Haddington.

The early history of St Mary's in the fifteenth and sixteenth centuries was closely associated with the thriving, bustling town of Haddington. Trade with countries far and wide in wool, cloth hides and fleeces, allied to the development of rich agricultural land in the Lothians, saw the townsfolk look to St Mary's, not only for the gratification of their spiritual needs, but also as a meeting place.

The two most important buildings in Haddington were the Tolbooth, opened in 1422 and in use until 1741, and St Mary's, completed in 1480 but in use for almost a hundred years before that. Whereas the former housed the Burgh Council, the Assize Court and a prison, and was therefore assigned to the more formal, regulated business of the area, St Mary's was used as a centre for day to day transactions, and was a place where deals could be struck. Notaries, men who were qualified to conduct the legal requirements of business, strode the floor of the church nave daily. This area in front of the High Altar was, for the most part, of furniture and furnishings and played host to the sound of intense conversations between agent and client.

Of course, whenever and wherever there is the sound of human voices and constant activity, there will be an attraction for others to attend also. Boys and girls came to join in the fun. Even dogs were allowed in.

Notwithstanding High Mass was sometimes ongoing, it was to a background of conversation and tumult. St Mary's was very much a social centre which the Tolbooth could not emulate.

From St Mary's, along Sidegate and then right up the High Street, there were stalls of every trade doing business. Candlemakers, tinsmiths, cordiners (shoemakers), bakers etc...were all trying desperately to make themselves heard. Haddington was a thriving town.

St Mary's itself was built on the site of a former church which had been destroyed by an invading English army. St. Michaels church in Linlithgow and St. Giles in Edinburgh were all built to a similar design, albeit the original architect is unknown. Each tower was surmounted by a crown steeple although, in the case of St. Mary's, it fell victim to the English guns during the siege of 1548-9. Following the siege, the English army removed the bells from the tower and carried them off to Durham.

The construction of St. Mary's began in 1380. In 1400 the church was consecrated and became a Collegiate Church. It is still the largest parish church in Scotland. People may ask "Why here? Surely large cathedrals or churches are usually found in the main cities?" What needs to be remembered is that in the fourteenth and fifteenth centuries when St Mary's was built, Haddington was one of the four largest towns in Scotland, along with Edinburgh, Aberdeen and Roxburgh (destroyed long ago.)

Mass was celebrated every day at the High Altar, notwithstanding the general hubbub which prevailed. What had originally been a simple service commemorating the Last Supper was now an elaborate ceremony. The bread and wine were blessed by the priest and signified the body and blood of Christ, so the entire ceremony was a re-enactment of his final sacrifice on the Cross and therefore of intense spiritual significance.

Thereafter the ringing of the Sanctus Bell, the lighting of altar candles and the dispensing of incense from censors swung by priests were of the utmost significance to those parishioners who were present. Merely taking part brought the likelihood of important benefits. Food would be plentiful and life long lasting. Angels would keep watch over them.

Dotted around the nave and choir areas were a total of seventeen altars most of which were dedicated to saints. It was common practice for a tradesman from the town to adopt an altar. The cordiners (shoemakers) favoured St.

Crispin whose feast day is the 25th October. The bakers adopted St. Aubert, the former bishop of Avranches who founded Mont St. Michel. The tinsmiths chose St. Eloi, also known as St. Eligius, the patron saint of goldsmiths and other metalworkers. He is best known as the patron saint of horses. The tailors opted for St. Anne, the mother of Mary and grandmother of Jesus. Other altars were dedicated to St. John, or John the Apostle as found in the Bible, St. Andrew, the Apostle and brother of Peter, St. Cuthbert, a monk, bishop and hermit who was saint of the early Northumbrian church, St. Michael the Archangel, St. Nicholas, also known as Nicholas of Myra (Turkey) and also as the "wonderworker," St. Ninian who was a missionary among the Picts in the eighth century, St. Peter, a former fisherman who became the first Apostle, St.Thomas, an early Apostle and St. Bartholomew who was also one of the Apostles.

There were also altars to St. Catherine, St. Serverus and St. Salvator.

It was common practice for parishioners, especially the more wealthy ones, to endow altars and arrange for Masses to be said at them upon their demise.

As the parishioners crowded around the dividing rood screen, once the Sanctus Bell had rung, their belief in the overwhelming importance of the service, being carried out in front of them, was tempered by the knowledge that the authority of the priests was secondary to the authority of the Burgh Council , operating from the Tolbooth a few streets away.

The volumes of old Council records cover the period 1424 to 1714.Effectively the bulk of information on display covers the two hundred years from immediately before the Battle of Flodden to the Act of Union and thus provides a fascinating background to well known events in Scotland during the period. The documents themselves lay at the bottom of an ancient wooden chest in the Town Clerk's Chambers in Haddington, without order or arrangement of any kind. They were, for the most part, in a very dilapidated condition from damp, neglect and other causes.

The text offers an insight into everyday life in Haddington for the two hundred years. The humdrum and trivial sit alongside the dramatic and famous, the beggar and vagrant vie for attention with the Provost and Lord. In particular, it is revealing to see the Reformation develop on a local, as well as an inter national, scale.

It is time now to let the extracts speak for themselves. The first words come from William Harpur's pen and are dated 28th May, 1426.

"John of Ford gave a silver chalice, weighing 8 pounds and 12 ounces, to St. Peter's Altar."

Thereafter reports of caring for altars in St. Mary's are a regular feature in Council records.

"July 30th 1454. Robert of Higaldiston, burgess of Haddington, with the full agreement of his spouse Annie, has provided, for the healing of all souls, ancestors' souls and successors' souls, and for all Christian souls, pure and perpetual alms to the Altar of St. John the Baptist in the parish of Haddington, and for a chaplain to say mass for the aforesaid souls, every Wednesday for evermore, an annual sum of twenty shillings, in the usual currency of Scotland, to be provided twice a year, i.e. Whitsunday and Martinmas in winter, from any portion or from the whole of his landholding plus appurtenances, lying in the said borough on the south side of Market Street between the land of Tom of Cockburn to the east "and the land of Henry Vaus on the west. An annual payment of thirteen shillings, raised from the said holding held in tenure to Our Lord the King, be paid to Our Lady's Altar in the parish of Haddington, and, to the heirs of John Bowmaker one merk. It is established that the said annual rent of twenty shillings shall be paid to the said Altar of St. John and to the chaplain for saying mass, together with all profits etc... resulting from the said annual rent, or which may apply in any manner or way in pure and perpetual alms, all of the aforesaid being paid annually without fraud or guile."

On the 2nd August 1454 – "Thomas Alanson, burgess of Haddington, with the full agreement of Margaret his spouse, gave, in pure and perpetual alms, fo the saving of his, his wife's and his children's souls, his ancestors' and his successors' souls, and all Christian souls and to St. Mary the Virgin and St. John the Baptist in the parish kirk of Haddington, in order that a chaplain be appointed to say mass for half a year, or for as long as it may last, the sum of forty shillings, in ther usual currency of Scotland, given twice a year at Whitsuntide and Martinmas in winter. To be raised from the rent from the whole of his landholding etc..."

On 1/2/1470 – "Sir John Young gave to the Altar of St. Michael the Archangel, situated in the parish kirk of Haddington, 5/5d from the rent of land lying to the west of

Hardgate, between the land of the late William Cruikshanks to the north, and the land of the late William Crumby to the south.

Also 15d from Stenton's land lying to the west of the cross between the land of the late Robert Crumby to the west and the common venell to the east. And this shall be raised and paid for the chaplain of the said Altar to pray for the souls of the late William Young and Elizabeth his wife, father and mother of the said Sir John Young and his soul after his demise. This placed before the Council by Laurence Fleming, Clerk and Scribe of the Court."

Finally, in this particular year of 1470 – "June 27th, 1470. John Patonson, burgess of Haddington, cordially gave, granted and discharged, perpetually and forever more, to the Altar of St. Michael the Archangel, in pure and perpetual alms, and annual rent of 18/4d in the usual currency of Scotland, to be raised annually at the two usual times of the year, Whitsuntide and Martinmas in winter, to be evenly apportioned from a landholding etc... which lies in the Borough of Haddington on the south side of Market Street, between the land of Robert Tod to the west and the land of Robert Lawson to the east, so that obituary service can be held for the soul of the said John Patonson, Laurence

Patonson his son, and for the souls of Libby Patonson, Janet Patonson and Marion Patonson, his daughters, and for his two wives' souls, and his ancestors' and successors' souls, and for all Christian souls, following the demise of the said John Patonson on the day of his anniversary with placebo and dirge and a solemn requiem mass to be sung be eleven Provosts and Clerks, and also as many masses as will be paid for out of 10/11d to be given to the poor folk as alms that day."

Sixty years later, the style of language changes, but the message remains – "This day the Assizes ordered that the craft of smiths should keep their Altar in a state of good repair as of old, and that they should have all of the privileges that they used to have. Or else the Altar shall be given to the town and all former privileges be revoked."

On July 4th, 1531 –"This day the Baileys, Council and members of the public, granted to the craft of shoemakers, the upkeep of the Crispin and St. Michael Altars in the High Kirk. Their master is to pay 1d per week; others serving in this task a halfpenny and bound apprentices one merk a year. Officials of the Council will impound the output of those who will not pay. This also applies to the self employed and apprentices."

On 5/11/1532 –"Which day the Baileys, Council and townsfolk ratified and affirmed the action to make bakers maintain the upkeep of their Altar. At which the chief official of the bakers complained to the Baileys of those who were the guilty parties and those who cursed him."

On 14/10/1537 –"William Duncan, Robert Duncan, James Cook, John Young, John Lowrie, David Lawson and all the other tailors decided, on behalf of themselves and their successors within the Burgh of Haddington, what name to use for their craft for the future. Also that 11s. should be paid for the upkeep of the Altar as all agreed."

Control of church finances and upkeep is also well documented in Council records e.g.- "6/2/1533 – Which day the Baileys, Council and townsfolk present instructed the bellringer to walk about the town himself, allowing no substitute, under penalty of losing his position. He was ordered to keep beggars and dogs out of the Kirk. He was entitled to half a merk for his fire and candle and be one of all Christian souls, and no more."

Also, "15/10/1538 – The Assize ordered the Kirk Master to find sufficient locks for his premises, to be inspected by the Baileys and Council."

Also, "31/7/1539 – Which day the Assize ordered that parish clerks to maintain the oil lamp that hangs in the choir. It should be lit at the second bell of Evensong and remain so until the Clerk locked the doors."

Appointments also fell within the Council, remit. At this time members of the Council were also chosen to form the Assize, so, in effect, it was the same group of people who administered the law of the land as well as the effective running of the town.

"30/6/1543 – The Council ordered the appointment of a Kirk Master-for the being Thomas Ponton was appointed, but for a year only. It was pointed that his wishes should be obeyed, as others have been previously.

Thomas Ponton declared that he would prepare only the usual accounts which the position required.

The Council ordered the Kirk Master not to exceed 11s. in purchases without the consent of the Baileys and Council."

The Kirk Master taught students in the Kirk during the day. Latin and theology, as it was known at the time, were the only subjects on offer.

Also, "23/6/1544 – Which day the Provost, Council and townsfolk were summoned by the handbell to convene in the Council House in order to award Sir Archibald Borthwick, Chaplain, the position of the Red Chaplaincy, within the College Kirk of Haddington, which was lying vacant following the death of Sir Patrick Mauchline, the previous Chaplain, together with a stall in the choir, all pledges, emoluments, profits, insignia and all other manner of gain which the late Sir Patrick Mauchline had before. This gift was ordered to be bestowed thereupon, under the Common Seal, as being appropriate.

The same day, the Provost, Council and townsfolk addressed all present and named Squire Adam Brown as Chaplain to the parish clerkship of Haddington, which position the said Sir Archibald Borthwick had held before. It was ordered that a presentation be made to that effect, under the Common Seal, as appropriate.

The Provost, Council and townsfolk gave to Squire Robert Simpson a pension of ten merks, which the said Adam brown had previously. It was to be given to him at the first service which he led, except the Red Service or St Katherine's. Alternatively he was to receive five merks, in addition to the previous ten merks, plus his stall in the

Choir. It was ordered that the gift was to be made under the common seal a appropriate.

The Provost, Council and townsfolk allocate the aforesaid service to the aforesaid persons who were to take up residence as required by the permanent fund, as long as they performed their duties as well as their predecessors."

Further instructions from Council on 26/11/1539. – "John Lauder was ordered to go to the Kirk on Lady Day." Also "3/10/1540. The Council ordered that the Baileys should instruct as many honest men as possible to go about with the Kirk collection plate, in their own time. Whoever was told to do so and refused should pay the same amount as he would normally pay on a Sunday plus 8s. unrefundable, to the Baileys. Every man should perform this duty unless there was a legitimate reason not to do so."

The "open door" policy, which the Kirk adopted from the start, had its drawbacks –"22/12/1544. Which day James Guthrie and Agnes Ogill, his spouse, were accused of stealing a certain urn from the Kirk in Haddington. They denied the charge and claimed that they received it from John Smith, who held it under warrant. This warrant was produced before the Court. They were told never to appear in town unless they could produce the warrant, failing which they might be sentenced to death by the Assize. It was further proclaimed that no man should receive them into his house, under similar penalty."

Finally "27/11/1545. No sick or unclean people were to be allowed to go to church; instead Mass would be held for them in St. Katherine's Chapel."

A blank appears in the records from which these extracts are taken, extending from December 30th, 1545 to March 15th, 1551 after which the extracts continue as before. The break may easily be accounted for as the stringent regulations which were shortly before the break promulgated by the Provost, Baileys, Council and community show us that the plague was raging in the town and neighbourhood.

Turmoil and war must also have afflicted the inhabitants at this time. As we see from entries referring to "ye captain of ye French Armye," the "Wynnings of ane blak horss fra ane Inglisman yat nyt Lord Bowes was takyn" and "furnishing of cartis to ye Kingis gounnes," the Earl of Hertford's invasion occurred about this period. Protector Somerset, still pursuing the "rough wooing" policy of his predecessor

Henry VIII, took and fortified Haddington in 1547 and retained possession until 1549.

Haddington suffered grievously, over the years, from its geographical position. Lying directly in the path of any invader marching on Edinburgh, it was sacked on several occasions, mainly by English armies. In the mid 1540s political developments down south reached the ears of the Burgh Council to their great alarm. Henry VIII, frustrated in his wish to marry off his son Edward to the Scots Princess, newly born in Linlithgow, was intent on sending north to enforce his wishes. The Burgh Council hurriedly made provision to ensure the Kirk silver, at least, was safe – "9/6/1545-Which day, the Provost and Baileys, acting on the advice of the Council, gave to George Kerrington a silver chalice belonging to St. Katherine's Altar, which bore -on its base the name of Richard Crumbie, together with a Cross, and on the chalice lid a hand. John Lawtery gave surety for its safe delivery.

Item- Delivered to Squire Thomas Mauchline a silver gilded chalice, inscribed at the base "This Chalice, St Marys of Haddington" –for Our Lady's Altar. John Lawtery gave surety for its sure delivery.

Item – Delivered to Sir John Fraser, the Trinity Chalice of silver, double gilded, inscribed at the base "The Trinity" with "Mr Robert Walterston" written above, together with his coat of arms, and, on the chalice lid "Jesus." Alexander Brown gave surety for its safe delivery.

Item – Delivered to Sir William Cockburn, St. John the Baptist's Chalice, silver gilded, inscribed on the base "Chalice of St. John, Church of Haddington." It had a Cross on the lid. Alexander Simpson gave surety for its safe delivery.

Item - Delivered to Sir Archibald Borthwick a silver chalice, having inscribed on the base a crucifix, and, in writing, "John of Crumbie and his spouse, sua me fiori Fecarutit" and on the lid "Jesus." William Brown, Provost, gave surety for its safe delivery.

Item – Delivered to Sir James Mauchline, curate of St. James, a silver chalice, inscribed on the base "St. James" with "William Kemp and his wife's mark, orate pro William Kemp et ejus spousa." On its lid was written "St. James." John Wilson gave surety for its safe delivery.

St Nicholas chalice was placed in the Common Chest.

Item-St. Ninian's chalice was placed under the care of Alexander Lawson.

Item –The High Altar was to be restored within eight days."

However, it was 1548 before the town was finally occupied by the invading English army. Earl Grey, the English commander in the field, place Sir James Wilsford in command of the Haddington garrison and ordered him to build a wall around the town. It was necessarily built of earth since the imminent arrival of French forces did not allow time for a stone construction. Those few townsfolk who had not already fled, pleaded that St Mary's and St Martin's should be spared. Wisford agreed and his guns left the two kirks alone. Unfortunately the French took advantage and assembled a large number of men behind St Mary's in preparation for an attack. They were spotted and an outraged Wilsford ordered the guns to fire on them.

Inevitably St. Mary's suffered grievously. The guns scored many hits, however inadvertently, on the Choir (chancel) half of the kirk in particular. The roof collapsed and great gaps appeared in the walls. Nothing daunted, the French built a wooden platform on the kirk tower from which they could fire directly down on to the besieged garrison. The

English fired back, causing yet more destruction. By the time the siege had ended, only the Nave half of the kirk remained more or less intact.

When the townsfolk returned from Edinburgh, or cellars deep beneath the ruins, they wept to see the devastation which met their eyes. Smoking, empty shells were all that remained of their houses and St Mary's presented a sorry sight.

It seemed like the end of everything they held most dear. In far off Eisleben, in Saxony, Martin Luther had begun the attack on Roman Catholicism. That too was lost. A fresh start to rebuilding Haddington would go hand in hand with a fresh start to the Church service.

Sir James Wilsford who fired on St Mary's.

PART TWO

PART TWO – 1550-1625.

In the first half of the sixteenth century events in Europe and England, as well as in Haddington itself, dramatically changed the church routine in St. Mary's.

Martin Luther, a German Protestant Reformer, drew up 95 theses protesting against the indulgences, as he termed them, of the priesthood in 1517. At the Diet of Worms, 1521, he refused to retract his charges levied against Rome. He followed up his act of defiance by translating the Bible into German. Thereafter his preaching of the Protestant view started a religious revolution throughout Europe.

In England, Henry VIII, 1509-1547, made himself Head of the Church of England following a disagreement with Rome over his wish to divorce Catherine of Aragon who proved unable to bear him a son. A nationwide suppression of the monasteries soon followed, and their estates were confiscated (1536-40). The rise of the English Reformation was soon under way.

In Scotland, George Wishart, 1513-46, who had studied under the Protestant Calvinists in Geneva and Germany, returned to Scotland to spread a new doctrine. John Knox became a follower of Wishart's preaching. Following a sermon in St Mary's, Wishart told Knox to remain in Haddington while he returned to Edinburgh. He was arrested, tried for heresy, and burned at the stake.

John Knox, born in Giffordgate, Haddington in 1513, fled to St. Andrew's after hearing of Wishart's arrest, only to be arrested himself. He spent the next nineteen months as a galley slave. Upon his release, he travelled to Geneva and studied Calvinism. He returned to Edinburgh in 1559 and was ordained as the Minister of St. Giles Cathedral. From this point on he became the chief inspiration and influence of the Scottish Reformation. Papal authority was abolished, the holding of a Mass forbidden and replaced by a Confession of Faith. In this way the Church in Scotland turned to Protestantism and an organisation framework which featured Elders, Kirk Sessions and a General Assembly.

Slow progress was made in repairing St Mary's following the siege of Haddington which ended in 1549. Given that the choir (chancel) was in ruins, such repairs as were possible were made to the nave. The temptation to make use of the many stones lying around the ruined choir proved too great to local householders who seized the opportunity to repair their own property. Even the Council used Kirk stones to repair the Nungate bridge.

Meanwhile Protestantism was growing steadily in Scotland. For too long, it seemed to the churchgoing public, they had been made to admire the colourful vestment adorning clergy and listen to Catholic liturgy, all of which failed to reflect their own lives. They considered they had little in common with priests and bishops who were never shy in refusing a flagon of wine, or a side of prime, home reared beef.

John Knox had a ready waiting appreciative audience when he breathed fire and brimstone against Popery from the pulpit. Local gentry in East Lothian were themselves attracted by the new approach adopted by these preachers like Knox who were prepared to risk charges of heresy.

John Knox's approach relied heavily on the Calvinism he had learnt in Geneva. It could be defined as a Protestant theological system developing the Lutheran doctrine of justification by faith alone, using an emphasis on the Grace of God. Crucially the system centres on the doctrine of Predestination i.e. is it heaven or hell for us?

As an approach it attracted heavy criticism from Lutherans and was seen as a real threat to Roman Catholicism. The counter attack cited the Bible itself as calling for the destruction of images while suggesting it was the huge increase in the sale of Bibles which had led to the creation of Calvinism in the first place.

Knox and his followers won the day and in 1560 the Reformation Parliament made Scotland officially a Protestant country. A major problem arose immediately when it became obvious that there were too few Protestant ministers to go round. The problem was solved by allowing Roman Catholic clergy to keep their positions, and their sources of remuneration, provided that they did not say Mass. Of course, the longstanding link between St. Andrews and St. Mary's was now broken and a new group, the Lords of Congregation, now dictated religious affairs in Scotland.

Even in its sorry state of repair St. Mary's continued to attract worshippers. To help matters, it is alleged that it was John Knox himself who suggested that a wall be built separating the ruined choir and transepts from the nave. This idea was quickly put into effect and the congregation could now take part in a service as a whole with ministers present alongside, rather than be made to peer through the detested rood at a garishly clad priest on the other side.

Patrick Cockburn was appointed as the first Protestant minister. His congregation sat on benches facing each other rather than having to stand. All altars, statues, paintings, vestments, Sanctus bells and incense were removed and were replaced by psalms and services (in English) and sermons. Communion was celebrated only four times a year.

The offices of the new system rose from three under Roman Catholicism to four – The Pastor who looked after the laity, formerly the role of the parish priest, the Doctor who was responsible for teaching at all levels, which included a scholarly investigation of the deeper meaning of Bible text, and the Elder who was given a disciplinary role in the Church via the Church Court. This exercised government by Committee or presbyteries, hence the use of the word Presbyterianism.

Finally came the Deacon who in Protestant circles was allotted the "dogsbody" role and was the lay officer.

On 29/4/1557 came the first step to tackling the thorny problem of altering the Church service-"Prebendaries of the

College Kirk of Haddington were summoned to appear at the Tolbooth on 6th May for consultation re the augmentation of the Divine service of the said Kirk."

Confining the church to the nave focussed the attention of those attending to repairs. The first mention in the Council reports occurred on 5/3 1555- "Which day Martin Wilson was summoned before the judges by the deacons and the craft of bakers to show where the chalice of St. Towbart's Altar was and whether it was repairable and to swear in judgment to tell the truth."

Progress was slow and the next mention does not appear until 11/7/1572 –"The Kirk windows, in front of the Fleshers' Altar, were to be made of glass. Rock steps were to be built in the Kirk yard to prevent livestock from entering . Four trees were to be planted."

John Knox, from a popular engraving (SW)

Later that year, on 6/11/1572 –"The Friar Kirk pavement was to be transferred to the High Kirk and relaid there."

"The Treasurer was instructed to buy timber for new seats and stairs in the Kirk, as well as a new pulpit."

On 14/12/1575 – "The windows above the table at the north side of the Kirk were to be washed and sprinkled with lime. Three windows on the south side of the Kirk were to be glassed and the rest washed and the rest of the doors

On the 4th April, 1576, -"The Treasurer would have the north and west side of the Kirk completed. The Pillar of Repentance would be demolished and remade in wood."

It would appear that the Kirk was now in a satisfactory condition. Repairs were completed and henceforth essential maintenance was all that needed to be carried out.

A new King, James II, proved to be an inspiration for a fresh development in St. Mary's –"8/6/1603 –Daniel, James and Lawrence, wrights, were hired to build one seat at the east end of the Kirk, stretching from the one already built by them at the north-east end of The Kirk, southwards to the southernmost pillar within the Kirk, with four rails in front to support it and one pair of brass supports fixed to the wall and sealed so that dust and dirt could not enter the Kirk.

Each pillar would be three feet wide with three seats each – the two hindmost being raised by one foot and a half more than the third. The four faces of the pillar would be panelled with a fine wainscot, with a moulding covering each two panels, so that the overall effect would be as good as any of the College Kirks of Edinburgh or Leith, with mouldings above and beneath. The front part of the back seats would be covered with fine wooden planks, each moulded as above. Each seat would have a flooring of wooden planks around it. One stairway and entry would be made of wood, and the entrance door would be fine oak wrought with panels, bands of wainscot, and with turned pillars at the top of each seat. Another entry would be made at the north end for the Provost to enter through. All would be completed by 1st July 1604. All wood would be provided by the wrights, except for the four trees already provided by the Treasurer. The total bill would be £100, payable as follows :the minimum required to be paid for the timber and delivery thereof, to be paid in cash, and the remainder to be paid on completion. If the work was completed to the satisfaction of the Council and Magistrates, a further 50 merks, over and above the £100, would be paid to the wrights.

The southern entry would be a wooden stair, clad in oak."

Thereafter repairs were carried out as needed. – "The Treasurer was instructed to rewire the west window of the Kirk .(6/12/1605)."

A stern message was to be found in the following record – "20/4/1609 – The Treasurer was instructed to have a new Pillar of Repentance built at the west end of the Kirk, to cope with the increasing number of adulterers and fornicators."

The increasing pressure placed by tradesmen on those in authority to ensure a physical presence in the Kirk was taken up on 4/6/1617 - "A request was received by the bakers and woodworkers of the Burgh, to build a seat at the west end of the Kirk, following the Act of Session (27/5/1617). It was proposed that, if the Burgh would provide two long trees to be placed between the west pillars, and four wainscot pillars to hold up the crossbeams, they would build the gallery to match other galleries and not affect the Samuelson Gallery, all at their own expense. A third part of the gallery was to be dedicated to the Burgh i.e.

James Carmichael and George Grier. The Treasurer was instructed to provide the said four pillars in fir and to fix the two joists at the expense of the Burgh."

Finally, on 20/9/1624 – "A petition was lodged by the Kirk Session to receive 400 merks from the Gentlemen of the Parish which they could offer to the Council as annual rent, provide that a slater and glassworker could mend the broken windows of the Kirk. The Council refused the offer."

Increasing evidence that shows the control that the Council held over the Kirk is found in records relating to payments, i.e. – "29/11/1571 –All rents due from Chaplaincies and Altars were to be collected and given to the Schoolmaster, or an assistant, to teach children, plus an Exortar (one appointed to give religious exhortation under a minister) in the Kirk, for which a qualified man was to be sought. Cuthbert Simpson disagreed with this, saying that it should be provided out of the Common Purse."

On 10/1/1572 –"James Carmichael, Minister, was awarded ten merks to pay his room rent for a year, starting from last Martinmas, 1571."

On 9/4/1572 –"All Chaplaincies and annual rents pertaining to the Kirk should be handed to the Curate, or Common Prayer Reader, who would also serve as Schoolmaster."

Problems arose from non-payment. On 3/4/1573 –"One third of the annual rent from the Kirk was to be set at default, while the Collector was to impound goods to the value of the other two thirds next term."Also, on 20/5/1572- "The Collector and Chaplains of the Kirk were ordered to pass through the streets of the Burgh and impound for annual rents due as necessary. Sir William Cockburn consented to the will of the Council re the annual rent due for St. John's Altar. Sir Alexander Henderson sought agreement on rent due."

On 7/4/1574 "Friar Fleck was to be paid ten merks for titles pertaining to the Kirk. Interest was to be collected from the estate of the late Alexander Simpson at the expense of the Burgh."

On 1/12/1574- "A charter of feu duty, made under the Common Seal of the Burgh, with sasine to follow , was granted to John Seton, Bailey, for the landholding formerly belonging to St. Crispin and St,. Crispin's Altar, for an annual rent of 13/4d, payable to the Treasurer."

Sometimes the Council were obliged to become involved in financial settlements involving Kirk personnel - "19/12/1578 –"the Treasurer was instructed to pay Andrew Darling, the Beadsman (one employed to pray for others) in the Magdalen Chapel, the sum of £10/12s, in the name of James Ponton, in settlement of a debt, in return for which the said Andrew would discharge him of the debt and refrain from further proceedings."

Wages were always falling behind -" 11/12/1587 –James Carmichael, Minister of God, was due to return to practice as previously (having been summoned to the service of King James). He was formerly accustomed to having his rent paid. Th Treasurer was instructed to pay him 20 merks p.a. and he was to find lodgings himself."

Also, on 24/12/1588 –"John Wilkie, Treasurer, was instructed to pay 100 merks to John Kerr, Schoolmaster, for services rendered as Minister of the Kirk. This sum was to be paid only when the Treasurer felt was the best time to do so."

On 16/11/1603 –"Alexander Seton, Treasurer, was granted £8/1s which had been spent by him on Minister's dinners in

Alexander Simpson's house at the time of the visit to the Kirk."

Purchases for the Kirk also came within the Council's remit- "3/1/1612 - The Treasurer was instructed for the Kirk Bible- £10/5/4d (in Scots money.)

The Council kept a watchful eye on money allocated to the Kirk –"10/11/1620 –Discussion took place about the £20 paid to James Carmichael, Minister, each year for house rent, since he had stopped visiting the sick."

Also, on 20/9/1624 –"The request of James Lawrie, Reader in the Parish Kirk of Haddington, to have his stipend increased to 50 merks, was refused by the whole Council who said that he did not make enough use of what he already had."

The Council reinforced its position over matters involving the Kirk by the way in which it dealt with a string of Kirk related offences – "7 /1/1557-Henry Campbell, Burgess, was accused of impeding John Douglas in the performance of his duty while impounding goods from the said Henry's house. He was also accused of swearing in St. Ninian's Chapel last Sunday in full view of a great multitude of people. John Ayton rang the town bell and accused Henry

Campbell before a judge of the High Court. Henry Campbell confessed. He was found guilty and sentenced to be punished by the Provost according to the law."

On 30/3/1570 –" Tenant farmers from the Vicarage were told that they must put no livestock in the Kirkyard, under penalty of forfeiture to the Burgh."

A more serious offence occurred on 23rd May, 1584 – "Adam Millar, cutler, was arrested for twice striking James Reid, Minister, with a sword, thereby drawing blood and causing him injury, which was admitted."

Presumably this case was referred to the High Court.

The Council produced new laws to regulate attendance at church – "18/10/1598. No merchants were to open booths at prayer time on Sundays. No idlers were to hang around the gate at prayer time. Each household, of more than three persons, should have at least one person at prayers; under penalty of 12d for a first offence and double for any repeat offence."

Throughout the entire period there was a continued need for appointments to be made. Continuous discussion in the

Tolbooth, and not the Church, considered suitable candidates for a variety of positions at St. Mary's.

Inevitably it was to the Treasurer that the task was assigned, beginning on 16/3/1563 –"The Treasurer was instructed to settle John Swyton in his clerical office, find a room for M. Patrick before next Whitsunday, and pay Andrew to clear up and lock the Kirk doors, and to find a basin for the administering of baptism, and to confiscate the fruits of the Vicarage until the tenant farmers pay a fee to the Guardian, which used to be paid to the Curate, and to refund Cuthbert Cockburn for the damage to his cornfields at the conclusion of the church service."

Occasionally applications were received from outside – "28/3/1566- Sir William Wilson petitioned to be restored to the position of Parish Clerk, which he formerly held between 1535 and 1559. Since all Clerks had been restored to their former office, he requested the same i.e. ministering at the Parish Kirk, using water at baptism ceremonies, keeping the Kirk clean, closing and opening the Kirk doors as necessary, and collecting the 12d. duty owed from each house in the Burgh. He had been born in Haddington and would be happy to serve, and to sing the psalms each Sunday, and act as Chanter.

It was agreed that 11s.p.a. would be awarded to Sir William Wilson for looking after the Kirk."

The above extract is an example of the "settling down" period following the incredible transition from Roman Catholic to Protestant service.

At times the search for suitable candidates needed to be spread further afield –" 30/3/1570 –John Ayton, Provost and Bernard Thomson, Bailey, were instructed to go to Edinburgh to search for a minister."

Occasionally, it was necessary to combine positions – Walter McConquell was appointed to read Common Prayers in the Kirk at 7 a.m. in the summer and 8 a.m. in the winter. He was to act as Clerk of Session on Sundays, Wednesdays and Fridays, and to teach in the school for a year. His pay at 50 merks p.a. payable at the two terms in equal portions."

Unfortunately this individual could not manage his position alone for long-"17/5/1577 –George Nesbit was hired to say prayers three days a week in the Kirk, i.e. Tuesdays, Thursdays and Fridays at 7.a.m. in the summer months and in winter at the appointed hour. He was also to serve as Assistant Schoolmaster for one year at 11 merks p.a. plus the use of a room."

More help was soon on its way –" 25/4/1578 – Lucas Wilson was appointed to be Reader of the Common Prayer during the daytime, and to serve as Assistant Schoolmaster for six months, commencing at Beltane. He was to be paid 25 merks, i.e. 12 merks 6/8d. per quarter, plus 4d per child."

Also –"3/9/1578- Henry Chapman was appointed as Kirk Reader and Assistant schoolmaster for six months, starting immediately, for a wage of 25 merks, i.e.12 merks 6/8d. 1/

The following extract from Council records includes the first reference to a school in the Burgh, as opposed to the Kirk. –"9/8/1592-George Sprot, son of the late Richard Sprot of Jedburgh, was appointed Doctor to the School. He was also required to lead the Psalms in the Kirk for one year, beginning at Hallowmass. He was to serve under John Callender, Master of the Grammar School, in teaching all the schoolchildren. He was to be paid 50 merks at the usual terms i.e.Hallowmass, Candlemass, Beltane and Lammas, in equal portions. William Henderson stood surety for him."

Appointments were also made for jobs outside the Kirk e.g.- "1/12/1598 –James Bowie was hired to ring the bells at Prayers, Preaching and Sessions. He was also to bury the corpses of the dead in graves seven feet deep. He was never to be found drunk, but to behave properly at work. He was also to dig graves for those executed. If he was found to be Conquell was to have the same fees as John Graham, his predecessor.

On 11/10/1605 "Because of the slowness of the workmen in repairing the Kirk steeple, Richard Wilson was appointed overseer to note how long they worked each day, how many days they were absent, and to report this information to the Council. The Treasurer was instructed to pay him 13/4d per week."

Finally, on 8/5/1622 –"James Lowrie, musician, was appointed to teach men and children to sing, take up the alms in the Kirk on a Sunday, with other prayers before and after the sermon, and each morning and evening .",

It seemed, towards the end of this period, that all was well in St. Mary's. The roofing had been repaired with slates, the walls were firm, strong and windproof. The windows were newly glassed and the floor of the nave newly laid with good planking. The Council could congratulate themselves on a job well done.

Within the Kirk, however, tensions were simmering. The ministers, James Carmichael and George Grier were appalled at the extent to which society had taken over, at how control was firmly in the hands of the Council. This drift to the secular had grown out of control, in their view. Grier, in particular, decided to take a firm stand.

The interior of the Kirk had taken on a bright, colourful appearance with the various trades each claiming a distinct place in the gallery built within the nave. Each trade proudly displayed their craft with banners depicting recognisable tools used everyday by them. The masons' banner showed a mortar and pestle, the tailors, a needle and thread, the cordiners (shoemakers) a pair of shoes, and so on. To Grier's eyes it was almost a reversion to the gaudy colours of Roman Catholic days.

He declared the whole sight to be intolerable and ordered its removal. Little did he realise the potential outcome of his action.

On the 8th October, 1612, Thomas Maislet was accused of wrongdoing against George Grier, Minister, by cursing and harassing him and generally misbehaving in the Parish. The said George Grier had reproved the said Thomas for not ringing the bells, or preaching or praying or any of the other duties normally carried out by him, as well as remaining in the Kirk during the whole of preaching time etc...The answer offered was that the said George was lying, which Thomas continued to argue. He was nevertheless found guilty of the offences and ordered to be put in irons and kept there during the magistrates' pleasure. Thereafter he was to be detained in custody until he had repented by public proclamation at the Kirk and the Market Cross or wherever George Grier decided; thereafter to perform further acts of repentance at the discretion of George Grier.

On 12/12/1614 –"John Vallance (younger) complained of being surrounded by bakers on Saturday, 10th December, in the evening. He was proceeding quietly to his own house from the house of his uncle, William Vallance, when two of the said craft came up to him from behind, one armed with a heavy staff and the other with a dagger, and attacked him, giving him several blows to the head before running off. He thought them to be John Kyle and William Main, bakers, who had been debarred from the rest of the craft. The two accused confessed, saying it was because their seat had been taken down by John Vallance, who, in their opinion, should have been pre-eminent in stopping this from happening. It was also stated that Walter Hogg and Mark Cockburn were lying in wait on the previous night to carry out a similar attack before James Cockburn returned home, this having been agreed by the four of them. More evidence was heard, following which, by a majority vote, it was found the Patrick Hogg, Deacon, Walter Hogg, Mark Cockburn, David Kyle, John Kyle, John Gray, William Black and William Main, all bakers, were guilty of the crime committed against John Vallance. They were ordered to be detained in custody, pending a decision on the punishment to be inflicted."

On 15/1/1615 –"William Main and John Kyle were ordered to be placed in irons, following which a great number of night, some armed with swords and some with heavy staves. Injuries were inflicted on passersby, who were not looking for trouble, after which it was ordered by the Judges that John Kyle and William Main be forbidden to walk the streets at night, carrying any kind of weapon ,unless on legitimate business, or going to or from their own homes. If they disobeyed they would be regarded as vagabonds and treated as such. No one was allowed to parade at night in the streets carrying a weapon, unless on legal business, on penalty of a £5 fine. Also, because of the great unrest caused in the Burgh by taking down the bakers' seat, it was ordered that, in future, no one should slander the magistrates for their action in this matter, or else they would be fined £10."

On 16/6/1615 –"William Stoddart, cutler, was accused of blasphemy and slander against George Grier, Kirk Minister and his wife, harassing him and vilifying the magistrates in the course of their duties. On the 13th June, the said William came to George Grier's house in his absence, and called out, in a loud voice, that he was a swine, a bumpkin, a vagabond and other blasphemous words, vowing that he would stab him and kill him, as well as calling his wife a harlot and a whore, all without reasonable cause, excepting the removal of the carpenters' seat, which was carried out with their consent, as well as that of noblemen, barons, gentlemen and others, so that there would be more space in the Kirk. He turned on those who had arrested him and told them to go and hang themselves, in a manner which demonstrated contempt for Our Sovereign Lord, his laws and authority, as well as his own oath of burgess-ship. He finally confessed, saying that he did not remember what he had said or done. He was ordered to be placed in the stocks at the Cross, as an example to others, and to offer public repentance in the

Kirk, and to be detained in custody until he had paid all the fines he had previously incurred."

In the case of James Carmichael events developed in a much more sinister way, however that lay ahead. There was no sign of any serious problems at the outset of his career in St.Mary's. Which is not to say that it was an easy introduction – far from it.

"15/11/1576 – James Carmichael was told by the Council that, considering his load as a Minister, another might be found to serve in the School, thus correcting previous failures if the Council to keep their promise to provide an assistant, which promise was neglected because of the frequency with which Councillors etc... were changed. Secondly, having already promised that the School would be based in the Burgh , and despite the false, malicious rumours raised by others, the progress towards this aim had been thwarted, therefore James Carmichael was not to blame for the disorder and inconvenience that has ensued. The Council would, therefore, take responsibility for dealing with the slander which has arisen. . Nevertheless, the Council desired James Carmichael to heed their plea, and if he did, the Council promised to select a qualified man, free from fault, heresy, papacy or idolatry, following the public pronouncement of Christ the Evangelist in the Realm. James Carmichael would then surrender the position of Schoolmaster, together with stipends, School fees etc. The Gift of the Abbey of Holyroodhouse, given by Adam, the holder of the benefice of the said Abbey, under the Common Seal of the Abbey, and with the King's confirmation, would be cancelled. Whereby James Carmichael, his heirs and assignees, would be recompensed in travel expenses to the sum of £100. Further, a debt of £20, owed by James Carmichael to the Council, would be wiped clean. £40 would be paid on the 25th December, a further £11 would be paid on Whitsunday, and the balance paid thereafter by James Cockburn, Treasurer. Adequate lodging would be provided for James Carmichael, rent free, in the Burgh, for as long as he stayed on as Minister. He would continue to help out in the School when necessary, and until a Master is found for all the schools except the High Grammar School.

Witnessed by Thomas Steven, Notary Public, Clerk of the Burgh of Haddington- in his own hand."

It would appear that James Carmichael continued as the sole Minister for some twenty years, barring the ten years betweb 1587-97 when he sought shelter in England from enraged foes ,before help was secured.-"21/7/1596 –From propositions put to them at the time of the Kirk visit on 20th July about finding a second Minister, bearing in mind that Hugh Chapman, the Reader, was old and frail and unable to carry out his duties any more, it was decided that the work could be done by two Ministers. Therefore, James Carmichael and a second Minister would remain at the Kirk to perform their daily service, and parishioners would be approached to make up a stipend for a second Minister. No Reader was to be appointed in future, and no glebe, house or manse would be needed, or any claim made on the Council by a second Minister. His stipend would be borne by the Parish rents, amounting to 100 merks."

On the 23rd May, 1598 Carmichael was again seeking the support of King James –"James Carmichael, Minister, was to travel to see the King, and the Officer to the Burghs, and other nobles, to seek support for the repairing of the Burgh, which was partly burnt down on 18th May. Thomas Spottiswood and Paul Lyle would ride with the Minister and Provost."

On the 12th June. 1598 –"Sir William Seton of Kylesmuir and Andrew Gray received the oath of James Carmichael,

Minister of God's Word at the Parish Kirk, and made him a burgess."

But there was another side to James Carmichael.

A young King James VI had sailed from Denmark with his bride only to be met by a huge storm, forcing them to take shelter in Norway. On resuming their voyage to Scotland they were again forced to endure gales and were fortunate to make land safely, but considerably stirred. An enquiry afterwards placed the blame firmly on the shoulders of witches. Formerly a non-believer, James's experience at sea changed his mind and he pursued the apprehension and persecution of witches vigorously.

He wrote a book entitled "Daemonologie" listing the actions and pursuits of witches. It is believed that he was helped considerably in his writing by James Carmichael, who may even have written most of the book. James was appointed "Witch Finder General" and instructed by the King to bring as many of the so-called "witches" to justice as quickly as possible.

To be fair to James Carmichael, many of the clergy throughout the length and breadth of the British Isles had been quietly nursing a considerable resentment at the turn of events which had resulted in the replacement of the Church at the forefront of society by secular authority. Suddenly, it seemed that the population took their instruction from Councils and the like, rather than Ministers.

So, this latest demand from the King himself offered a golden opportunity to reverse matters. The Church would now conduct investigations into a nationwide scourge i.e. witchcraft.

James Carmichael wasted no time in carrying out the King's instructions. In 1590 there began a two year trial in North Berwick of about 70 people suspected of having taken part in the practice of witchcraft. Prosecutions were carried out in the Old Tolbooth, Edinburgh, and, invariably, torture of suspects followed. Among the techniques used were a) the witches bridle, an iron mask with sharp points to penetrate the unfortunate's face, b) stretching on the rack, c) being forced to wear a boot which could be stretched to crush the prisoner's foot d) having fingernails pulled out, and e) being enclosed in a chair which was then lowered into a lake until such time as a confession was literally "wrung" out of the prisoner, or the drowning of the unfortunate, which was taken to mean that a verdict of "not guilty" applied.

At the North Berwick trial those accused included the Earl of Bothwell, old Agnes Sampson (80) from Humbie, Agnes Thomson from Edinburgh, Barbara Napier from Angus, Dr. Fean (John Cunningham) a Prestonpans schoolmaster, Euphemia Maclean, Gillie Duncan from Tranent, Robert Grierson, and Lennit Bandilands. All were tortured and several burned at the stake, including Gillie Duncan, Agnes Thomson and John Cunningham. The Earl of Bothwell managed to escape the vengeance of the prosecutors. They claimed that the accused were working in tune with the Devil, so they were only performing the will of God.

Altogether 3-4000 were designated as witches in Scotland between 1560 and 1707, the year of the Act of Union with England. Following the conclusion of the North Berwick trial, James Carmichael became aware of a rising tide of disapproval amongst both his parishioners and the upper classes, and deemed it a prudent move to take a prolonged sabbatical of ten years, mainly in England.

So ended the witchfinding career of James Carmichael, Minister of St. Mary's College Church in Haddington, Man of God.

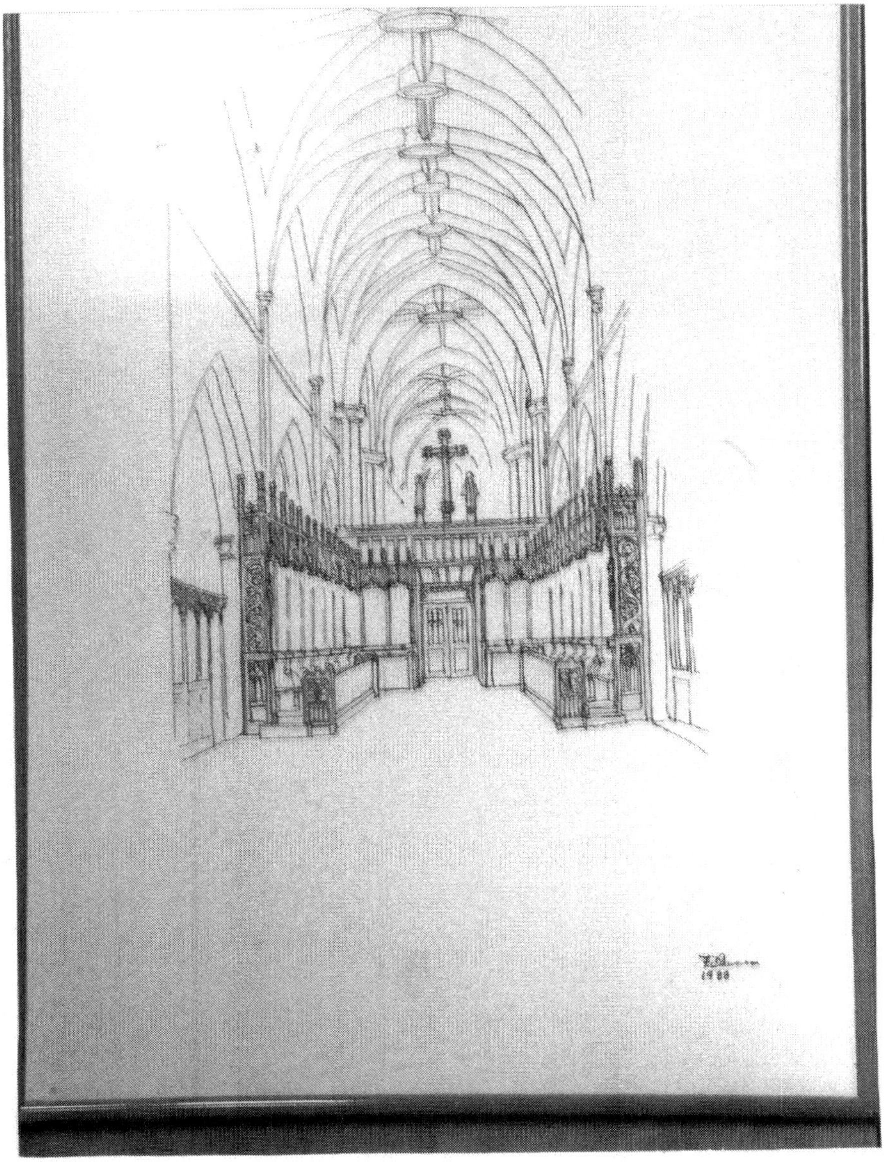

PART THREE

St Mary's in its ruined state.

PART THREE -1626-1700.

The years between 1625 and 1650 are not available in Haddington Council records. Nationally it was a time of intense conflict in all parts of the British Isles. Having come to the throne of England on the death of his father, Charles 1st clung to the out dated concept of "The Divine Right Of Kings," conveniently setting aside Magna Carta. In Scotland he wished to revert to a near-Roman Catholic liturgy, with bishops and regalia. The Scottish people were not having it.

At a service in St. Giles, Edinburgh, on the 23rd of July,1637 , with the Dean of Edinburgh about to introduce the Bishop of Edinburgh to speak, a market stall holder, Jenny Geddes stood up and shouted "devil give you colic on your stomach, false thief, dare you say Mass in my ear," before hurling her stool at the startled Dean's head. Pandemonium broke out.

There ensued a period of conflict between the king's forces and the Covenanter army – a period known as the two "Bishop's Wars."

The first was inconclusive but the second saw the King's army totally defeated, with the Covenanters advancing into England as far as Durham.

The Covenanters' pledge was to God alone. They held a contract with God, a direct relationship with no King's interference or Papistry. Over 300,000 joined in a condemnation of the Episcopal system of Church government. Instead a Church of Scotland was formed which was entirely independent of the King.

A National Covenant was formulated in 1638. After the Bishops' Wars the Covenanters became the "de facto" government in Scotland and remained so until Cromwell roundly defeated the Scottish army supporting Charles II at Worcester in 1650.

The years of King Charles Ist's reign, and beyond, saw continuous upheaval within the Protestant ranks. Argument and discussion, followed by the development of new stances was the order of the day. It was as if Protestantism was not enough, it had to be scrutinised and redefined time after time.

Among the many splinter movements were the Baptists who believed that baptism could be performed by professing believers only and must feature complete immersion. The Anabaptist belief was that baptism was possible only when the candidate confesses a faith in Christ Jesus and did not apply to infants.

Seventh Day Adventists were a Protestant Christian denomination distinguished by an observance of Saturday, not Sunday, as the true Sabbath, it being the seventh day of the week in the Christian and Jewish calendar. They emphasised and professed a belief in the second coming of Christ Jesus.

Plymouth Brethren was shown to be a conservative, low church, non-conformist Evangelical Christian movement which held the Bible to be the supreme authority for Church doctrine.

Methodism was the belief put forward by John Wesley. It places a focus on the sanctification and the effect of faith on a Christian. It offers an assurance of salvation, an imparted righteousness, a perfection in love, the works of piety, and the primacy of the Scripture. It features a strong support for all works of Charity, including support for the sick, poor and afflicted.

The Protestant hope that it could replace Roman Catholicism entirely proved to be misplaced. Dissension within its own ranks saw, as described above, many other groups dispute their primacy. The main threat, however, lay with a series of monarchs who wished to retain bishops even if the service was changed. A new creation of Episcopacy would take its place among the religious practices of Scotland

In 1582 the Scottish Episcopal Church emerged on to the scene. The Church of Scotland had previously rejected Episcopal government and adopted a Presbyterian one, run by elders. A contest began where Monarchs of Scotland fought to reintroduce bishops while the population resisted and turned their attention elsewhere.

In 1584 James VI had his way, The Scottish Parliament passed the "Black Acts" which saw the appointment of two bishops and placed the Church of Scotland under his control. This move produced uproar in the streets, forcing him to concede that it should be the General Assembly who would dictate church affairs. In 1603, James stopped meetings of the General Assembly and increased the number of bishops. In Perth in 1618 a new General Assembly published "Five articles of Episcopalian Practice," a move greeted with almost total disdain in Scottish congregations.

Further tinkering with church services served only to alienate them. The Restoration of the Monarchy in 1660 brought about the re-imposition of Episcopacy causing further conflict. It was not until 1689 that Presbyterian practice was finally re-established within the Church of Scotland. The year following saw the Comprehension Act which allowed Episcopalian bishops to hold on to their rights of tenure, stipends etc... once they had taken the Oath of Allegiance.

Throughout all of these years of religious turmoil, the congregation of St. Mary's remained faithful to the Presbyterian code, as if the hand of John Knox still held power. In 1642, when Charles 1st had alienated the English Parliament to such an extent that Civil War broke out, St Mary's was considering local issues. According to Church records, on the 15th May, Elizabeth Watson brought before the Church Session the serious case of disobedience on the part of her daughter, Jean. After consideration, Jean was ordered to be obedient to her mother "according to the Law of God."

William Main petitioned the Church Session, in the name of the rest of his brethren, the shoemakers of Haddington, to design a room in the Kirk "that they might build one seat for them and one for their servants." So much for George Grier!

This plea was followed up and investigated. John Ayton, Bailey, reported that he had "carried out a survey of the Kirk yesterday morning and found that one seat might be built in the room directly beneath that of the hammermen." Therefore the Session duly allocated that place for the shoemakers to build a seat for their members.

Another case involving mother and daughter was reported to the Session, which found that Isobel Anderson and her daughter were accused of "flyting" (quarrelling) and were both severely rebuked.

Most of the rest of the Church records (carefully written out by the Session Clerk in his own handwriting) refers to charity handouts to the poor and needy of the town. Various payments were made to "James and Elizabeth Young, to Bessie Blaikie, to the blind boy in Poldrate, to William and Bessie Donaldson, to the poor in Drem etc...etc..."

Such matters were previously the concern of the Burgh Council, operating from the Tolbooth. It appears that the Council decided that they had more important things to deal with, and were therefore content to let the church Session take over, a further illustration of how the two authorities were drifting further and further apart.

One concession which the Tolbooth authority made was to allow the bell on the Tolbooth tower be used to announce Kirk services, the bells of St. Mary's having been removed by the English army during the Siege of Haddington. The Tolbooth big bell was used to warn the townsfolk of the imminent Kirk service while smaller handbells were rung outside the Kirk to remind those in the vicinity.

The larger Tolbooth bell was used regularly i.e. every day in the town for many purposes, including early morning and to announce significant events. Accordingly it needed regular maintenance and replacement when it was no longer fit for purpose e.g."James Oliphant was instructed to bring back an eleven pound bell, for which he would pay the Customs duty. For each pound that the bell weighed, nine "Nobles" would be sung at the Feast of Martinmas."

Sometime later "A bell was ordered from William Mayne which the Treasurer would pay for, setting aside four merks for the cost of his –"burgess-ship. The bell was to be hung at the west end of the Tolbooth as quickly as possible."

As in all human activities, some perform better than others, while some don't seem to bother e.g."Since the bell ringing and clock maintenance in the Burgh had not been kept up because of the sloth of James Bowie, the incumbent keeper of the position, it was decided to find an honest man for the job."

The ravages of time, of course, saw even cast iron bells fail to perform their function very well e.g."The two old bells, one the old Knox bell which was broken and the other in good condition, were to be recast as one. William Main, potter, agreed to carry out the task."

Also, on 19th March, 1700 "The Great Bell in the Tolbooth was to be removed and recast. It would be replaced, temporarily, by a smaller bell."

A strange case was brought to light on 8th March, 1616.- "William Sinclair, bellringer, was accused of breaking into fresh graves, especially that of John Ayton's sister while she was not yet fully decomposed nor fit to be seen, and for interring there strangers and outsiders. He was ordered to be placed in the stocks for a full day, and thereafter to be held in custody pending sentence."

All of the above are extracts from Haddington Burgh Council records relating to the St.Mary's Kirk and its bells, or lack of them. To return to the Kirk itself, other matters raised covered a whole range of issues. To start with, on 21st March, 1657 –"The Council ordered the undermanagers to be removed from the Council pew in the Kirk. Any unauthorised person was forbidden to occupy a Council pew, these being reserved for Council members and magistrates." Obviously democracy did not extend to Kirk attendance. Then a returning issue appeared on 18th January, 1658- " The Provost was to go to Edinburgh to seek advice on what to do about Margaret Anderson, confined at the time in the Tolbooth, and, if possible, to get a warrant transferring her to Edinburgh."Evidently he was successful, because, on the 15th February, "The four men, who escorted Margaret Anderson to Edinburgh, were to be paid two merks each." It appears that Margaret Anderson was suspected of witchcraft.

On the 24th January, 1659, the Council returned to more familiar territory-"The Provost, Patrick Young and David Wilson, plus the Clerk, were to decide on Robert Kerr's stipend, based on the acreage bought by the Burgh from the Earl of Haddington."

On the 15th September, 1659 –"It was decided that as many stones as were needed should be taken from the Old Kirk to repair the bridge etc..." Restoring the stonework of the Kirk accurately was going to be almost impossible in the future.

On the 28th May, 1662 –"The Colours were to be run up and the militia called to arms. They would assemble after the sermon on Sunday, under the usual penalty for non-attendance." Which suggests that Kirk attendance was mandatory, at least for the military.

On the 25th January, 1665 –" The Council unanimously approved the appointment of Robert Watson, Precentor of the Tron Kirk in Edinburgh, to be Precentor of the Parish Kirk in Haddington, following the death of William Brown, at the same fees, duties and housing allowances. This was to be confirmed following his appearance at the Council." A Precentor was someone who led the singing i.e. a choirmaster. It is to be noted that the Council were still appointing Kirk officers.

Following on from his appointment –"Robert Watson was also appointed Master of the Music School, to teach men and children to sing and play instruments. It would be open to those outwith the Burgh as well as residents. He was to take up Psalms on Sunday, as well as before and after sermons, to read prayers every weekday morning and on Sunday before the sermon. He was to read the Scripture before the sermon a.m. and p.m. He was provided with a house, rent-free, and paid £100, plus a further fee from the Kirk Session."

The Council was still anxious to find exactly what was owed to them by the Kirk. On the 12th April, 1673 – "The Charter Chest was to be searched for a contract between the Earl of Haddington and the Burgh about the disposition of the Tithes, the Parsonage and the Vicarage in the Burgh acreage, and all other papers relating thereto, and of payment of an annuity or taxes therefrom."

Investigations carried out enabled the Council to announce on 7th June, 1673 –"An Act was passed about the right granted by the Earl of Haddington to the Burgh, for the Tithes for the Parsonage and the Vicarage."

By now Charles II had gone, to be replaced by James VII and II. The first recorded action which the Council unrtook with regard to the Kirk was on 26th December, 1687 – "William McCall and John Sleich, Magistrates, the Treasurer and the Clerk, were to meet property owners and scour records in order to raise taxes with which to repair the Parish Kirk and build the second Minister's Manse."

Also, on 17th April 1688- " Alexander Maitland's expenses were allowed for consulting advocates about the tax levy for repairing the Kirk, and building for the second Minister, which amounted to £23/11s."

Evidently the matter was still to be settled, and on 18th May, 1691 –"The Council convened, along with several landowners of the Parish, before the Lords Mersington, Fountainhall and Presmennan, to decide the levels of payment to repair the Kirk. It was agreed that the Burgh would pay one-fifth and the landowners the rest. This agreement served only to restore the present exigency and was not to be regarded as binding in future years."

Finally, on the 5th November, 1694 –"The Council approved and vouched for James Forman, Minister, against whom an action for libel had been raised by the united Presbyteries of Haddington and Dunbar. He was cited to appear before the Synod in Edinburgh to answer the charge. William McCall, Provost, Richard Millar and John Robertson, Baileys, were to accompany him in a show of solidarity, and to read out the address given previously by the Presbytery in his support."

Evidently James Forman, although an Episcopalian, was successful in his defence against the charge because he continued to serve as Minister of St Mary's until 1702.

St Mary's

CONCLUSION

CONCLUSION

In all of the years which have come and go since the Act of Union (1707), St. Mary's has continued to remain as the centre of religious activity in Haddington. Other churches and faiths have sprung up which have their followers but all recognise the dominance of the Kirk by the river, the Lamp of Lothian and Haddington's link with Scottish history.

Two world wars, floods, disasters and controversy have all come to pass before finally, in 1973 a restoration of the church shell was completed and St Mary's resumed its former appearance and glory. The choir (or chancel) was rebuilt with stone obtained from local quarries and a new polystyrene ceiling installed which matches the existing nave ceiling perfectly. As a gesture of friendship, the English returned the original bells so that they could "ring in" the second millennium.

S Mary's has survived the transition from Roman Catholic to Protestant and its congregation remain committed Presbyterians. Controversy has seen the discussion and arguments over sexual equality by the appointment of a female Minister. Meanwhile the graveyard surrounding the

Kirk has extended to all sides and beyond with St Martin's being adopted to cope with the overload.

In the town outside, society has drifted over the years to become increasingly secular. St Mary's is now allowed to run its own affairs without interference. The Tolbooth itself, a long lasting symbol of Council authority, was taken down in 1741, to be replaced, as a building only to be used by Council officials until the John Muir Centre was built in the 20th century.

The galleries (lofts) have long been removed. Today's Kirk now as long rows of pews to seat the congregation. Bodily comfort is provided by an effective heating system while re-designed entrances keep out the draughts.

The finance to pay for these improvements comes from weekly collections, contributions, donations and from a large list of events, concerts etc... which a paying public can enjoy.

A visitor to St Mary's is inevitably left awestruck at its soaring tower, its vaulted ceiling, the magnificent stone walls and beautiful stained windows. Long ago, master masons and their helpers built a structure which far surpassed anything they had achieved before. They wanted to build a House of God.

And He still dwells here. Amen.

THE END.

INDEX

A	PAGE NUMBER
Aberdeen	9
Act of Session	36
Act of Union	11
Alanson T	13
Anderson I	64
Anderson M	67
Assize Court	7
Avranches	10
Ayton J	40,43,64,66

B

Bakers	10
Bandilands L	53

B (contd)   PAGE NUMBER

Bishops War	59,66
Black Acts	62
Blaikie B	64
Black W	41
Borthwick A	18, 22
Bothwell	53
Bowes	20
Bowie J	44,66
Bowmaker J	15
Brown A	18,22
Brown W	22,68
Burgh Council	7,11,21,64,66

C

Callender T	44
C (contd)	PAGE NUMBER
Calvinism	27,28,29,30
Campbell H	40,41
Carmichael J	37,39,40,46,50,51,52,53,54,55
Catherine of Aragon	27
Chapman H	52
Chapman M	44
Charles 1st	39,63
Charles II	60,69
Christ Jesus	9,10,61
Clark A	4
Cockburn C	42
Cockburn J	12,48.58

Cockburn M	48
Cockburn P	31
Cockburn W	23,38
C (contd)	PAGE NUMBER
Comprehension Act	63
Cook J	16
Cordiners	9
Covenanters	59,60
Cromwell	60
Cruickshanks W	14
Crumby J	22
Crumby R	14,21
Crumby W	14

D

Darling A	39

Donaldson W	6,64
Douglas J	40
Duncan G	55
D (contd)	PAGE NUMBER
Duncan R	16
Duncan W	16
Durham	8, 69

E

Earl of Haddington	69
East Lothian	4,29
Edinburgh	9,28,35,54,59
Edward	21
Eisleben	24
Exortar	37

F

Fean	55
Fleck	38

F (contd)	PAGE NUMBER
Flemyng L	4,14
Fleshers Altar	22
Flodden	11
Ford J	12
Forman J	70
Fountainhill	70
Fraser J	22

G

Geddes J	59
Geneva	28,29
Giffordgate	6,28

Graham J	45
Gray A	52
Gray J	48
G (contd)	PAGE NUMBER
Grey	23
Grier G	37,46,47,49,63
Grierson R	55
Guthrie J	19

H

Harpar W	4,12
Henderson A	38
Henderson W	44
Henry VIII	21,27
Hertford	20
Higaldiston R	12

High Altar	7,9,22
High Mass	7
High Street	8
H (contd)	PAGE NUMBER
Hogg P	48
Hogg W	48
Holyrood	51

I (None)

J

James I and VI	34,39,53,62
James II and VII	69
John Muir Centre	74

K

Kemp W	22
Kerr J	39
Kerr R	67
K (contd)	PAGE NUMBER
Kerrington G	51
Knox J	6,28,29,30,33,63
Kyle D	48
Kyle J	47,48

Lamp of Lothian	73
Lauder J	19
Laurie J	40
Lawson A	23
Lawson D	16
Lawson R	14

Lawtery J	21
Leith	35
Linlithgow	8,21
L (contd)	PAGE NUMBER
Lords of Congregation	30
Lowrie J	16,45
Luther M	21, 24
Lyle P	52

M	
MacLean C	55
Magdalen	29
Magna Carta	55
Main W	47,48,63,65,66
Maislet T	66
Maitland A	69

Market Street	12,14
Mary	10
Mauchline J	2
M (contd)	**PAGE NUMBER**
Mauchline P	18
Mauchline T	21
McCall W	69, 70
McConquell W	45
Mersington	70
Methodism	61
Millar A	41
Millar R	70
Mont St. Michel	10
Myra	10

N	**PAGE NUMBER**

Napier B	55
Nesbit G	43
North Berwick	54, 55
O	PAGE NUMBER
Ogill A	19
Oliphant J	63

P

Patonson J	14,15
Patonson L	15
Patonson M	15

Q (None)

R

Reformation	11,28

Reid J	41
Restoration	63
Robertson J	70
R (contd)	**PAGE NUMBER**
Roman Catholicism	5,6,24,30,43,59,61,74
Rome	27
Roxburgh	9

S

Saint – Andrew 10,Anne 10,Aubert 10,Bartholomew 10,Catherine 10,18,20,21,Crispin 10,15,38,Cuthbert 10,Eloi 10,Giles 8,28,59,James 22,John 10,12,13,17,22,38Martin 23,Mary 13,Michael 8,10,13,14,15, Nicholas 10,22,Ninian 10,23,40,Peter 10,12, Salvator 10, Serverus 10, Thomas 10,Taubert 32.

Sampson A	55
Samuelson	36
Sanctus Bell	9,11,31

Seton A	39
Seton J	38
Seton W	52
S (contd)	**PAGE NUMBER**
Seventh Day Adventists	61
Sidegate	8
Simpson A	4, 38, 40
Smpson C	37
Sinclair W	66
Sleich J	69
Smith J	19
Somerset	20
Spottiswood J	52
Sprot G	44
Stenton	14
Steven J	51

Stoddart W	49
Swyton J	42

T

Tailors	10,16
Thomson A	55
Thomson B	43
Tinsmiths	10
Tod R	14
Tolbooth	7,8,32,64,65,74

U (None)

V

Vallance J	47,48
Vallance W	47

Vaus H	12
W	
Waterson R	22
W (contd)	PAGE NUMBER
Watson E	63
Watson J	67
Watson R	68
Wesley J	61
Wilkie J	39
Wilsford J	23,25
Wishart G	5,27,28
Wilson D	67
Wilson J	22
Wilson L	44
Wilson M	32
Wilson R	45

Wilson W	42,43
Worcester	60
Worms, Diet of	27
Y	**PAGE NUMBER**
Young J	12,14,16, 64
Young P	67
Young W	14

Made in the USA
Columbia, SC
17 November 2017